WHAT SHALL WE HAVE FOR DINNER?

SATISFACTORILY ANSWERED BY NUMEROUS

BILLS OF FARE

FOR FROM TWO TO EIGHTEEN PERSONS.

BY

LADY MARIA CLUTTERBUCK.

A NEW EDITION.

LONDON:

BRADBURY & EVANS, 11, BOUVERIE STREET.

1852.

INTRODUCTION.

THE late Sir Jonas Clutterbuck had, in addition to a host of other virtues, a very good appetite and an excellent digestion; to those endowments I was indebted (though some years the junior of my revered husband) for many hours of connubial happiness.

Sir Jonas was not a *gourmand,* although a man of great gastronomical experience. Richmond never saw him more than once a month, and he was as rare a visitor to Blackwall and Greenwich. Of course he attended most of the corporation dinners as a matter of duty (having been elected alderman in 1839), and now and then partook of a turtle feast at some celebrated place in the city; but these were only exceptions, his general practice being to dine at home; and I am consoled in believing that my attention to the requirements of his appetite secured me the possession of his esteem until the last.

My experience in the confidences of many of my female friends tells me, alas! that others are not so

happy in their domestic relations as I was. That
their daily life is embittered by the consciousness
that a delicacy forgotten or misapplied; a surplus-
age of cold mutton or a redundancy of chops; are
gradually making the Club more attractive than
the Home, and rendering " business in the city "
of more frequent occurrence than it used to be in
the earlier days of their connubial experience; while
the ever-recurring inquiry of

WHAT SHALL WE HAVE FOR DINNER?

makes the matutinal meal a time to dread, only
exceeded in its terrors by the more awful hour of
dinner!

It is to rescue many fair friends from such
domestic suffering, that I have consented to give to
the world

THE BILLS OF FARE

which met with the approval of Sir Jonas Clutterbuck, believing that by a constant reference to
them, an easy solution may be obtained to that
most difficult of questions,—" WHAT SHALL WE
HAVE FOR DINNER ? "

M. C.

CONTENTS.

——◆——

————————————

₀ The Appendix contains Receipts for some dishes, the preparation of which may not be generally understood.

WHAT SHALL WE HAVE FOR DINNER ?

BILLS OF FARE FOR TWO OR THREE PERSONS.

Giblet Soup.

Loin of Mutton, rechauffé à la Soyer. Mashed and
Fried Potatoes. Beetroot Salad.

Cold Mince Pies.

[Jan. to Dec.]

Fried Whitings.

Roast Loin of Mutton. Cauliflowers. Potatoes.

Toasted Cheese. Water Cresses.

[Jan. to Dec.]

Vegetable Soup.

Pork Cutlets, with Savoury Sauce.   Spinach.
Mashed and Brown Potatoes.

Bloaters.

[Jan. to Dec.]

B

Roast Ribs of Beef, rolled.   Brown Potatoes.
Spinach.

Rice Pudding.

[Jan. to Dec.]

Roast Fowl.   Bacon.   Hashed Mutton.   Mashed
and Brown Potatoes.

Roll Jam Pudding.   Macaroni.

[Jan. to Dec.]

Fried Sole.   Shrimp Sauce.

Haricot Mutton.   Mashed and Brown Potatoes.

Tartlets.   Omelette.

[Jan. to Dec.]

Veal Cutlets.   Hand of Pickled Pork.   Mashed
and Brown Potatoes.   Turnip Tops.

Marmalade Tartlets.

[Jan. to Dec.]

Roast Shoulder of Mutton.   Onion Sauce.   Browned
Potatoes.   Spinach.

Toasted Cheese.

[Jan. to Dec.]

Roast Leg of Welsh Mutton.   Spinach.   Mashed
and Brown Potatoes.

Macaroni.

[Jan. to Dec.

Lobster Cutlets.

Rabbit Curry.   Rice Dumpling.   Mashed and Brown Potatoes.

Italian Cream.

[Jan. to Dec.]

Vegetable Soup.

Minced Beef with Bacon.   Cold Pigeon Pie. Potatoes.

[Jan. to Dec.]

Roast Fillet of Mutton, stuffed.   Potatoes.

Currant Pudding.

Toasted Cheese.   Water Cresses.

[Jan. to Dec.]

Soles, with Brown Gravy.

Roast Loin of Mutton.   Rissols of Beef.   Mashed Turnips.   Potatoes.

Macaroni.   Broiled Mushrooms.

[Jan. to Dec.]

Roast Leg of Mutton.   Mashed Turnips.   Potatoes.

Suet Dumplings.

Toasted Cheese.   Water Cresses.

[Jan. to Dec.]

Sole in Brown Gravy.

Cold Beef. Salad. Potatoes.

Batter Pudding.

Toasted Cheese. Water Cresses.

[Jan. to Dec.]

Ox-Tail Soup.

Minced Mutton, with Bacon. Cold ditto. Mashed
and Fried Potatoes.

Strawberry Jam Cream.

[Jan. to Dec.]

Mutton Broth.

Roast Fowl. Boiled Bacon. Minced Mutton.
French Beans. Potatoes.

Cold Ground Rice Pudding.

Toasted Cheese. Water Cresses.

[Jan. to Dec.]

Ox-Tail Soup.

Stewed Veal. Cold Saddle of Mutton. Beetroot
Salad. Mashed and Brown Potatoes.

Eve's Pudding.

[Jan. to Dec.]

Ox-Tail Soup.

Fried Sole. Shrimp Sauce.

Haricot. Mashed Potatoes. Rice.

[Jan. to Dec.]

Giblet Soup.

Minced Mutton, with Bacon. Cold ditto. Mashed
and Fried Potatoes. Beetroot and Celery Salad.

Boiled Batter Pudding.

[Jan. to Dec.]

Vegetable Soup.

Bubble and Squeak.

Cold Beef. Hashed Hare. Mashed and Brown
Potatoes.

Rice Pudding.

[Jan. to Dec.]

Broiled Mackerel.

Stewed Rump Steak, with Vegetables. Mashed
and Brown Potatoes.

Bread-and-Butter Pudding.

[April to Aug.]

Fried Oysters. Lamb's Head and Minced Liver.
Mashed Potatoes.

Macaroni.

[April to Sept.]

Broiled Salmon. Shrimp Sauce.

Cold Lamb. Salad. New Potatoes.

Rice Blancmange. Italian Cream.

Toasted Cheese.

[April to Oct.]

Hashed Mutton, with Vegetables.

Roast Duck.   Green Peas.   New Potatoes.
Batter Pudding.   Artichokes.

Water Cresses.

[April to July.]

Pickled Salmon.

Calves' Liver and Bacon. French Beans. Potatoes.

Plum Pudding.

Macaroni.

[April to Sept.]

Broiled Salmon.   Shrimp Sauce.

Lambs' Hearts.   Cauliflower.   Potatoes.

Cold Ground Rice Pudding, flavoured with
Marmalade.

Toasted Cheese.   Water Cresses.

[April to Sept.

Broiled Salmon.   Shrimp Sauce.

Roast Fillet of Beef, stuffed.   Cauliflower.
Potatoes.

Baked Bread-and-Butter Pudding.

Cheese.   Water Cresses.

[April to Oct.]

Lamb Stewed with Peas.   Potatoes.

Batter Pudding.

Toasted Cheese.   Water Cresses.

[May to Aug.]

Steak.   Horse Radish Sauce.   Cold Lamb.   Salad.

Mashed Potatoes.

Rice Pudding.

Macaroni.

[May to Sept.]

Broiled Mackerel.

Minced Mutton, with Bacon.   Pork Cutlets.

Turnip Tops.   Mashed and Brown Potatoes.

Roll Jam Pudding.

Toasted Cheese.

[May to Sept.

Roast Leg of Lamb.   Salad.   Mashed Potatoes.

Sea Kale.

Omelette.

[May to Oct.]

Fried Whitings.   Shrimp Sauce.

Lamb's Fry.   Mashed and Brown Potatoes.

Macaroni.

[All the Summer.]

Fried Soles and Whitings. Shrimp Sauce.
Mutton Curry. Potatoes. Summer Cabbage.
Toasted Cheese.
[All the Summer.]

Broiled Mackerel.
Veal Cutlets. Bacon. Salad. Mashed and Brown Potatoes.
Fruit Pudding.
[All the Summer.]

Roast Leg of Mutton. Mashed and Brown Potatoes. Summer Cabbage.
Cold Custard Pudding.
Macaroni.
[All the Summer.]

Minced Beef, with Bacon. Cold Lamb. Salad. Mashed and Brown Potatoes.
Omelette.
[All the Summer.]

Broiled Mackerel.
Cold Lamb. Patties. Salad. Potatoes. Brocoli au Gratin.
[All the Summer.]

Lamb's Fry.   Fillet of Beef.   Peas.   New Potatoes.
Baked Rice Pudding.

[All the Summer.]

Fried Sole.   Shrimp Sauce.
Lamb's Fry.   Asparagus.   New Potatoes.

[All the Summer.]

Minced Collops.   Cold Lamb.   Beetroot Salad.
New Potatoes.
Raspberry Jam Sandwiches.

[All the Summer.]

Lamb's Head and Minced Liver.   New Potatoes.
Custard Pudding.

[May to Sept.]

Green Pea Soup.
Roast Leg of Lamb.   New Potatoes.   Asparagus.
Sweet Omelette.   Macaroni.

[May to Sept.]

Roast Leg of Lamb.   Asparagus.   New Potatoes.

[May to Aug.]

Green Pea Soup.

Minced Mutton.   Cold Mutton.   Patties.   Salad.
Potatoes.

Tartlets.

[May to Aug.]

Green Pea Soup.

Pickled Salmon.

Mutton Chops.   Hashed Venison.   Cold Bath Chap.
Peas.   Potatoes.

Cold Lemon Pudding.

Toasted Cheese.   Water Cresses.

[May to Oct.]

Stewed Lamb, with Peas.   Potatoes.

Black Currant Pudding.

Sweet Omelette.

[May to July.]

Vegetable Soup.

Fried Oysters.

Mutton Curry.   Rice.   Cold Beef.   Salad.   French
Beans.   Potatoes.

Apple Pudding.

Macaroni.   Water Cresses.

[May to Dec.]

Fried Oysters.

Veal Cutlets. Boiled Knuckles of Ham. Potatoes.
Cauliflower.

Toasted Cheese. Water Cresses.

[May to Aug.]

Brill.

Haricot Mutton. French Beans. Potatoes.

Ground Rice Pudding.

Prawns. Water Cresses.

[May to Sept.]

Pickled Salmon. Whiting.

Stewed Rump Steak. French Beans. Potatoes.

Rice and Apples.

Toasted Cheese. Water Cresses.

[May to July.]

Roast Shoulder of Mutton. Onion Sauce. Browned
Potatoes. Summer Cabbage.

Omelette.

[June.]

Baked and Stuffed Haddock.

Lamb's Head and Mince. Summer Cabbage.
Potatoes.

Cream Cheese.

[June to Aug.]

Rump Steaks à la Soyer.   French Beans.
Potatoes boiled.

Macaroni.   Water Cresses.

[July to Sept.]

Cod.   Oyster Sauce.

Rump Steak Puddings, with Oysters and Kidneys.
Potatoes.   French Beans.

Toasted Cheese and Water Cresses.

[July to Feb.]

Mutton Chops.   Broiled Mushrooms.   Grouse.
Potatoes.   Cauliflower.

Omelette.   Water Cresses.

[Aug. to Dec.]

Codling.   Oyster Sauce.

Grouse Pie.   Potatoes.   Mutton Cutlets.

Apples and Rice.

Macaroni.   Water Cresses.

[Aug. to Dec.]

Filletted Sole à la Maître d'Hôtel.

Haricot Mutton.   Potatoes.   Cold Grouse Pie.

Prawns.   Water Cresses.

[Aug. to Dec.]

Fried Oysters.

Irish Stew.

Toasted Cheese.

[Aug. to May.]

Fried Oysters.

Rump Steaks. Horse Radish Sauce. Mashed and
Brown Potatoes. Spinach.

Toasted Cheese.

[Aug. to Jan.]

Fried Sole. Shrimp Sauce.

Rump Steak à la Soyer. Hashed Hare. Potatoes.
Cauliflower.

Prawns. Water Cresses.

[Aug. to Jan.]

Fried Sole and Whitings.

Roast Leveret. French Beans. Potatoes.

Omelette. Water Cresses.

[Aug. to Jan.]

Roast Hare. Cold Rump Steak Pie. Mashed
Potatoes.

Rice. Roll Jam Pudding.

[Aug. to Jan.]

Cod rechauffé.

Broiled Turkey Legs. Cold Beef. Beetroot and
Celery Salad. Mashed and Brown Potatoes.

Plum Pudding.

[Aug. to April.]

Ox-Tail Soup.

Mutton Chops. Roast Black-Cock. Potato Balls.

Toasted Cheese.

[Aug. to Dec.]

Cod. Oyster Sauce.

Lark Pie. Potatoes. Pork Cutlets.

[Sept. to Jan.]

Fried Sole and Whitings. Shrimp Sauce.

Roast Hare. Potato Balls.

Macaroni.

[Sept. to Jan.]

Mutton Broth. Boiled Mutton. Hashed Hare.
Mashed Potatoes. Mashed Turnips.

Apples and Rice.

[Sept. to Jan.]

Carrot Soup.

Broiled Legs of Turkey. Cold Beef. Mashed
and Fried Potatoes.

Charlotte Brosse.

[Sept. to Feb.]

Mutton Chops.   Mashed and Brown Potatoes.
Roast Larks.

Apples and Rice.

[Sept. to Jan.]

Mutton Chops.   Roast Pheasant.   Fried Potatoes.
Roll Jam Pudding.

[Oct. to Feb.]

Carrot Soup.
Cold Saddle of Mutton.   Beetroot and Celery
Salad.   Fried Potatoes.
Roast Pheasant.

Bloaters.

[Oct. to Jan.]

Rump Steaks.   Roast Pheasant.   Potatoes à la
Maître d'Hôtel.

[Oct. to Feb.]

BILLS OF FARE FOR FOUR OR FIVE PERSONS.

Roast Loin of Mutton. Browned Potatoes. Salad.

Rice Blancmange, with Strawberry Jam and
Cream.

Toasted Cheese.

[Jan. to Dec.]

Fried Oysters.

Haricot Mutton.   Mashed and Brown Potatoes.
Roast Fowls.

Raspberry Puffs.

Stilton Cheese.

[Jan. to Dec.]

Carrot Soup.   Irish Stew.

Savoury Omelette.

Toasted Cheese.

[Jan. to Dec.]

Fried Sole.   Shrimp Sauce.

Mutton Cutlets.   Salad.   Mashed and Brown
Potatoes.

Cheesecakes.   Macaroni.

[Jan. to Dec.]

Filletted Soles.   Shrimp Sauce.

Minced Lamb. Calves' Liver and Bacon. Potatoes.
Cauliflower.

Pound Puddings.

Water Cresses.

[Jan. to Dec.]

• Vegetable Soup.

Fried Soles.

Roast Beef. Yorkshire Pudding.   French Beans.
Potatoes.

Toasted Cheese. Water Cresses.

[Jan. to Dec.

Mutton Chops. Broiled Fowl.   Potatoes.
Broiled Mushrooms.

Tapioca Pudding.

Bloaters. Water Cresses.

[Jan. to Dec.]

Fried Oysters.

Roast Beef. Yorkshire Pudding. Mashed and
Brown Potatoes.   Brocoli.

Macaroni. Water Cresses.

[Jan. to Dec.]

c

Mutton Broth.

Cold Beef.   Minced ditto, with Bacon.   Mashed
and Fried Potatoes.   Salad.

Marrow Pudding.

Bloaters.

[Jan. to Dec.]

Fried Soles.   Shrimp Sauce.

Roast Fillet of Beef, stuffed.   Turnip Tops.
Mashed and Brown Potatoes.

Spanish Pudding.

Toasted Cheese.

[Jan. to Dec.]

Fried Soles.   Shrimp Sauce.

Irish Stew.

Toasted Cheese.

[Jan. to Dec.]

Fried Sole and Whiting.   Shrimp Sauce.

Roast Leg of Mutton.   Salad.   Browned Potatoes.

Mince Pies.

Macaroni.

[Jan. to Dec.]

Vegetable Soup.

Roast Leg of Welsh Mutton. Pork Cutlets.
Salad. Mashed and Brown Potatoes.

Roll Jam Pudding.

Stilton Cheese.

[Jan. to Dec.]

Vegetable Soup.

Roast Loin of Mutton. Spanish Onions. Mashed
and Brown Potatoes.

.Apple Tart. Macaroni.

[Jan. to Dec.]

Baked and Stuffed Haddocks.

Broiled Fowl, with Mushrooms. Minced Collops.
Mashed and Brown Potatoes.

Raspberry Jam Sandwiches.

[Jan. to Dec.]

Salt Fish. Egg Sauce. Parsnips.

Cold Beef. Salad. Mashed and Brown Potatoes.

Marmalade Tartlets.

Toasted Cheese.

[Feb. to May.]
c 2

Salmon. Asparagus Soup.   Smelts.

Fore Quarter of Lamb.   Fricassee Chickens.
New Potatoes. Peas.

Lobster Patties.

Noyau Jelly.   Ice Pudding.

[May to July.]

Asparagus Soup.

Salmon Curry à la Soyer.

Cold Mutton. Minced Collops. Mashed Potatoes.
Salad.   Sweet Omelette.

Brocoli au Gratin à la Soyer.

[May to Aug.]

Asparagus Soup.

Turbot.   Shrimp Sauce.

Roast Saddle of Mutton. Stewed Pigeons. Mashed
and Brown Potatoes. Brocoli. Salad.

Pound Puddings.   Macaroni.

[May to Aug.]

Baked Haddock.

Roast Leg of Lamb. Stewed Kidneys. Peas.
Potatoes. Salad.

Cherry Tart.   Macaroni.

[May to Aug.]

Fried Soles.   Shrimp Sauce.
Roast Ribs of Lamb.   Peas.   Potatoes.
Roll Jam Pudding.

[May to Aug.]

Codling.   Oyster Sauce.
Beef Steak Pudding, with Kidney and Oysters.
Broiled Fowl.   French Beans.   Potatoes.
Plum Tart.
Toasted Cheese.   Water Cresses.

[May to Aug.]

Salmon.   Shrimp Sauce.
Roast Fowl.   Boiled Knuckle of Ham.   Sheep's
Hearts, stuffed.   French Beans.   Potatoes.
Batter Pudding.
Water Cresses.

[May to Aug.]

Salmon.   Shrimp Sauce.
Roast Beef.   Cauliflower.   Potatoes.
Greengage Tart.   Hominy.
Cheese.   Water Cresses.

[May to Aug.]

Asparagus Soup.

Fried Soles.   Shrimp Sauce.

Pork Cutlets.   Oyster Curry.   Rice.   Cold Lamb.
Salad.   Mashed and Brown Potatoes.

Marmalade Tartlets.

Macaroni.

[May to Aug.]

Brill.   Shrimp Sauce.

Mutton Cutlets.   Brussels Sprouts.   Potatoes.

Boiled Batter Pudding.

Bloaters.

[June to Oct.]

Filletted Soles.   Shrimp Sauce.

Roast and Stuffed Leg of Mutton.   French Beans.
Potatoes.

Greengage Tartlet.   Macaroni.

[June to Sept.]

Baked Haddock.

Roast Shoulder of Lamb.   Cauliflower.   Potatoes.
Broiled Mushrooms.

Saxe Gotha Pudding.

[July to Jan.]

Cod. Oyster Sauce.

Haricot Mutton. Roast Hare. French Beans.
Potatoes.

Apple Tart.

Toasted Cheese. Water Cresses.

[July to Jan.]

Cod. Oyster Sauce.

Roast Loin of Mutton. Stewed Rump Steak.
French Beans. Potatoes.

Damson Pudding. Macaroni.

[July to Oct.]

Cod. Oyster Sauce.

Haricot. Mashed and Brown Potatoes.
Macaroni.

[Aug. to Feb.]

Cod rechauffé with Potatoes.

Mutton Curry. Rice. Mashed and Brown Potatoes.
Apple Pudding.

[Aug. to Feb.]

Fried Whitings. Shrimp Sauce.

Mutton Chops. Mashed Potatoes. Beetroot Salad.
Brace of Partridges.

Apple Pudding.

Bloaters.

[Sept. to Feb.]

Fried Whitings.

Rump Steak à la Soyer.   Brace of Partridges.
French Beans.   Potatoes.

Tapioca Pudding.

Toasted Cheese.   Water Cresses.

[Sept. to Jan.]

Roast Loin of Mutton.   Mashed Turnips.   Mashed
and Brown Potatoes.
Woodcocks.

Pancakes.   Toasted Cheese.

[Sept. to Feb.]

Fried Whitings.   Shrimp Sauce.

Roast Leg of Mutton, stuffed with Oysters.
French Beans.   Potatoes.   Partridge.

Apple Pudding.

Toasted Cheese.   Water Cresses.

[Sept. to Feb.]

Haricot Mutton.   Roast Hare.   Mashed Potatoes.
Bread-and-Butter Pudding.

[Sept. to Jan.]

Cold Oysters.   Ox-Tail Soup.   Turbot.

Saddle of Welsh Mutton.   Veal Cutlet.   Tomato
Sauce.   Vegetables.

Cabinet Pudding.   Savoury Omelette.

[All the Winter.]

Vermicelli Soup.   Potatoes.   Salmon.
Lobster Sauce.

Saddle of Mutton.   Brocoli.   Potatoes.   Rabbit Pie.
Raspberry Jam Pudding.

Toasted Cheese.   Salad.

[All the Winter.]

BILLS OF FARE FOR SIX OR SEVEN PERSONS.

Vegetable Soup.

Roast Fillet of Veal.   Boiled Knuckle of Ham.
Greens.   Browned Potatoes.

Apple Tart.   Custards.

[Jan. to Dec

Scotch Mutton Broth.

Fresh Herrings.

Roast Shoulder of Mutton, Onion Sauce.   Curried
Oysters.

Roll Jam Pudding.

Toasted Cheese.

[Jan. to Dec.]

Cod.   Oyster Sauce.

Mutton, stewed with Vegetables.   French Beans.
Potatoes.

Baked Rice Pudding.   Savoury Omelette.

[Jan. to Dec.]

Fried Soles.   Shrimp Sauce.

Roast Haunch of Mutton.   Mashed and Brown
Potatoes.   Brocoli.

Apple Tart.   Custard.

[Jan. to Dec.]

Vegetable Soup.

Filletted Soles.   Shrimp Sauce.

Roast Leg of Mutton, stuffed with Oysters.
Minced Collops.   Spinach.   Mashed and Brown
Potatoes.

Cold Lemon Pudding.   Bloaters.

[Jan. to Dec.]

Boiled Mackerel.

Roast Leg of Welsh Mutton.   Minced Collops.
Spinach.   Mashed and Brown Potatoes.

Marmalade Tartlets.   Macaroni.

[April to Aug.]

Broiled Mackerel.

Veal Cutlets.   Bacon.   Cold Beef.   Spanish Salad.
Mashed and Brown Potatoes.   Cauliflower.

Rice and Apples.   Macaroni.

[April to Sept.]

Vegetable Soup.

Filletted Sole à la Maître d'Hôtel.

Roast Fillet of Beef.   Cold Pigeon Pie.   Salad.
New Potatoes.   Spinach.

Raspberry Jam Tartlet.   Custard.   Macaroni.

[May to Sept.]

Asparagus Soup.

Fried Soles.   Shrimp Sauce.

Patties.   Lobster Cutlets.   Curry.   Rice.
Cold Lamb.   Salad.   Potatoes.

Punch Jelly.

Toasted Cheese.

[May to July.]

Salmon.

Roast Loin of Mutton.   Boiled Fowls.   Bacon.
French Beans.   Potatoes.   Salad.

Greengage Tart.   Macaroni.

[May to Aug.]

Asparagus Soup.

Filletted Sole.   Shrimp Sauce.

Saddle of Mutton.   Mayonnaise of Fowl.
Cauliflower.   New Potatoes.

Gooseberry Tart.   Devonshire Cream.

Macaroni.

[May to July.]

Asparagus Soup.

Salmon.   Shrimp Sauce.

Roast Saddle of Mutton.   Rabbit Curry.   Rice.
Salad.   Sea Kale.   Mashed Potatoes.

Cabinet Pudding.   Macaroni.

[May to July.]

Carrot Soup.

Filletted Sole à la Maître d'Hôtel.

Roast Leg of Lamb.   Minced Collops.   Salad.
Mashed and Brown Potatoes.

Cold Lemon Pudding.

Toasted Cheese.

[June to Sept.]

Filletted Soles.   Shrimp Sauce.

Roast Leg of Lamb.   Stewed Rump Steak, with
Vegetables.

Cauliflower.   Potatoes.   Salad.

Currant and Raspberry Tart.   Macaroni.

[June to Sept.]

Filletted Soles.   Shrimp Sauce.

Roast Beef.   Cold Pigeon Pie.   Peas.   Potatoes.
Salad.

Raspberry and Currant Tart.   Macaroni.

[June to Aug.]

Fried Flounders.   Shrimp Sauce.

Rump Steak Pudding, with Oysters and Kidneys.
Bubble and Squeak.   Cold Beef.
Mashed and Brown Potatoes.   French Beans.

Boiled Batter Pudding.

Toasted Cheese.   Water Cresses.

[June to Sept.]

Fried Sole.   Shrimp Sauce.
Roast Leg of Lamb.   Peas.   New Potatoes.
Prince Albert's Pudding.
[June to Sept.]

Brill.   Shrimp Sauce.
Roast Rump Steak, rolled and stuffed.   Boiled
Rabbits.   Onion Sauce.
Potatoes.   Brussels Sprouts.
Lemon Pudding.
Toasted Cheese.   Water Cresses.
[June to Dec.]

Brill.   Shrimp Sauce.
Roast Loin of Mutton.   Beef Steak Pudding, with
Kidneys and Oysters. French Beans.   Potatoes.
Boiled Rice and Apples.   Macaroni.
[June to Dec.]

Vegetable Soup.
Codling.   Oyster Sauce.
Roast Fillet of Mutton, stuffed.   Cauliflower.
Potatoes.
Raspberry and Currant Tart.   Macaroni.
[July to Dec.]

Cod. Oyster Sauce.

Roast Rolled Ribs of Beef. Roast Fowl. Bacon.
French Beans. Potatoes.

Plum Tart.

Toasted Cheese. Water Cresses.

[July to Dec.]

Cod. Oyster Sauce.

Roast Loin of Mutton. Stewed Kidneys.
Mashed and Brown Potatoes.
Stewed Mushrooms.

Apple Pudding. Macaroni.

[Aug. to Feb.]

Cod rechauffé, with Potatoes.

Roast Beef. Pork Cutlets. Spinach. Mashed
and Brown Potatoes.

Bread-and-Butter Pudding.

Toasted Cheese. Water Cresses.

[Aug. to Feb.]

Filletted Sole. Shrimp Sauce.

Roast Beef. Haricot Mutton. Cauliflowers.
Mashed and Brown Potatoes.

Apple Tart. Custards.

Toasted Cheese. Water Cresses.

[Aug. to March.]

Vegetable Soup.

Baked and Stuffed Haddock.

Roast Saddle of Mutton.   Hashed Hare.
Brocoli.   Browned Potatoes.

Pound Puddings.   Greengage Tartlet.   Custard.
Macaroni.

[Sept. to Feb.]

Fried Soles.

Irish Stew.   Rump Steak à la Soyer.   Potatoes.
Brussels Sprouts.

Raspberry Jam Sandwiches.

Toasted Cheese.   Water Cresses.

[Sept. to March.]

Carrot Soup.

Filletted Soles à la Maître d'Hôtel.

Roast Saddle of Mutton.   Jugged Hare.
Spinach.   Mashed and Brown Potatoes.
Beetroot and Celery Salad.

Rice Blancmange.   Cream Tartlets.

Macaroni, with Bacon.

[Sept. to March.]

Pea Soup.

Filletted Soles.   Shrimp Sauce.

Roast Turkey.   Sausages.   Cold Ham.   Mashed
and Brown Potatoes.   Brocoli.

Open Damson Tartlet.   Macaroni.

[Sept. to Feb.]

Fresh Herrings.
Roast Leg of Mutton, stuffed with Oysters.
Stewed Kidneys.
Mashed Turnips.   Mashed and Brown Potatoes.
Greengage Tart.   Macaroni, with Bacon.

[Oct. to Feb.]

Oyster Soup.   Hare Soup,   Cod's Head.   Smelts.
Two Roast Fowls.   Boiled Bacon.
Saddle of Welsh Mutton.   Two Pheasants.
Eve's Pudding.   Raspberry Jam Tart.
Macaroni.

[All the Winter.]

Mock Turtle.   Cod's Head.   Smelts.
Roast Turkey.   Sausages.   Maintenon Cutlets.
Sweetbreads.   Mushroom Sauce.   Vegetables.
Apple Tart.   Orange Fritters.

[All the Winter.]

Turbot.   Lobster Sauce.   Fried Soles.
Shrimp Sauce.
Roast Pig.   Oyster Patties.   Fricandeau of Veal.
Mutton Cutlets.   Curry Rabbit.   Roast Beef.
Apple Fritters.   Macaroni.   Sweet Omelettes.
Croquits of Rice.

[All the Winter.]

D

BILLS OF FARE FOR EIGHT OR TEN PERSONS.

Vegetable Soup.

Fried Sole.   Shrimp Sauce.

Roast Fillet of Beef, stuffed.   Minced Mutton,
with Bacon. Browned Potatoes. Kalecannon.

Savoury Omelette.   Raspberry Jam Sandwiches.

[Jan. to Dec.]

Turbot.   Shrimp Sauce.

Roast Loin of Mutton.   Pigeon Pie.   Brocoli.
Mashed Potatoes.   Salad.

College Puddings.

Macaroni.

[Jan. to Dec]

Scotch Mutton Broth.

Fried Oysters.   Shoulder of Mutton.   Boiled Fowl.
Bacon.   Mashed and Brown Potatoes.
Stewed Onions.   Salad.

Batter Pudding.   Macaroni, with Bacon.

[Jan. to Dec.]

Filletted Soles.   Shrimp Sauce.

Boiled Beef.   Mutton Curry.   Rice.   Potatoes.
Kalecannon.

Ground Rice Pudding, flavoured with Marmalade.

Cauliflower au Gratin.   Water Cresses.

[Jan. to Dec.]

Barley Broth.

Fried Whitings.   Shrimp Sauce.

Roast Beef. Minced Veal. Cold Ham. Cauliflower.
Mashed and Brown Potatoes.

Bread-and-Butter Pudding.   Macaroni.

[Jan. to Dec.]

Roast Fillet of Veal.   Boiled Knuckle of Ham.
Mutton Pie.   Mashed and Brown Potatoes.
Spinach.

Roll Jam Pudding.

Toasted Cheese.   Water Cresses.

[Jan. to Dec.]

Carrot Soup.

Turbot.   Shrimp Sauce.   Lobster Patties.

Stewed Kidneys.   Roast Saddle of Mutton.   Boiled
Turkey.   Knuckle of Ham.   Mashed and Brown
Potatoes.   Stewed Onions.   Salad.

Cabinet Puddings.   Rice Blancmange, and
Cream.   Macaroni.

[Jan. to Dec.]

D 2

Green Pea Soup.

Salmon.   Shrimp Sauce.   Cucumber.

Veal and Ham Patties.   Lamb's Fry.   Roast Saddle
of Mutton.   Boiled Fowl and Tongue.   Asparagus.
New Potatoes.   Salad.

Gooseberry Tart.   Devonshire Cream.

Cabinet Pudding.   Macaroni.

[May to Aug.]

Ox-Tail Soup.

Cod.   Oyster Sauce.

Roast Saddle of Mutton.   Stewed Breast of Veal.
Stewed Onions.   Artichokes.   Mashed and
Brown Potatoes.

Eve's Pudding.   Raspberry Jam Sandwiches.
Custards.   Macaroni.

[Sept. to March.]

Green Pea Soup.

Salmon.   Shrimp Sauce.   Salad.

Haunch of Venison.   Boiled Fowl.   Pig's Jaw,
garnished with Beans.   Potatoes.   French Beans.

Lemon Pudding.   Raspberry and Currant Tart.

Devonshire Cream.   Macaroni, with Bacon.

[May to Sept.]

Green Pea Soup.

Salmon. Lobster Sauce. Cucumbers.

Lamb's Fry. Patties. Roast Saddle of Mutton.
Boiled Fowls. Peas. Potatoes. Salad.

Cabinet Pudding. Raspberry and Currant Tart.
Devonshire Cream.

Dressed Crab.

[May to Aug.]

Carrot Soup.

Turbot. Shrimp Sauce.

Roast Beef. Turkey Poult. Tongue. Patties.
Pork Cutlets. Stewed Celery. Mashed and
Brown Potatoes. Greens.

Hare. Macaroni.

Ice Pudding. Clear Jelly. Cream.

Cheese. Anchovies. Celery and Beetroot Salad.

[Aug. to Jan.]

Ox-Tail Soup.

Cod. Oyster Sauce.

Roast Saddle of Mutton. Pork Cutlets.
Kalecannon. Mashed and Brown Potatoes. Roast
Pheasants. Salad.

Soufflet Pudding. Mince Pies.

Anchovy Toast.

[Oct. to Feb.]

Scotch Mutton Broth.

Roast Goose. Mutton Curry. Rice. Cold Pigeon
Pie. Salad. Brocoli. Mashed Potatoes.

Eve's Pudding.

Toasted Cheese. Water Cresses.

[Sept. to Jan.]

Scotch Mutton Broth.

Roast Leg of Mutton, stuffed with Oysters.
Boiled Fowls. Knuckle of Ham. Cauliflower.
Mashed and Brown Potatoes.

Damson Tart. Macaroni. Water Cresses.

[Sept. to March.]

Vegetable Soup.

Brill. Shrimp Sauce.

Roast Saddle of Mutton. Minced Collops. Peas.
New Potatoes. Salad.

Currant Tart. Cream. Macaroni.

[May to Aug.]

Giblet Soup.

Baked and Stuffed Haddocks.

Roast Haunch of Mutton. Stewed Onions.

Browned Potatoes.

Roast Pheasant.

Pound Puddings.

[Oct. to Feb.]

Filletted Soles.   Shrimp Sauce.

Boiled Beef.   Roast Hare.   Carrots.   Potatoes.

Swiss Pudding.   Macaroni.

[Aug. to Feb.]

Cod.   Oyster Sauce.

Roast Leg of Mutton with Veal Stuffing.

Boiled Fowl.   Tongue.   Brocoli.   Mashed and Brown Potatoes.

Rice Blancmange.   Cream.   Macaroni.

[Nov. to March.]

Spring Soup.   Ox-Tail.

Salmon.   Lobster Sauce.   Mackerel à la Maître d'Hôtel.   Parsley and Butter.   Soles.   Potatoes.

Two Boiled Spring Chickens.   Asparagus Sauce.
Lobster Curry.   Sweetbreads.
Fore Quarter of Lamb.   Tongue.   Veal Olives.
Oyster Patties.   Two Ducklings.
Peas.   New Potatoes.   Asparagus.

Currant and Raspberry Tart.   Cold Custards.
Lemon Jelly and Charlotte Russe.

[All the Summer.]

Ox-Tail Soup.

Cod. Oyster Sauce.

Roast Saddle of Mutton. Pork Cutlets. Mashed
and Brown Potatoes. Artichokes.

Cabinet Pudding. Macaroni.

[Nov. to March.]

Spring Soup. Mock Turtle.

. Salmon. Fillets of Soles à la Maître d'Hôtel.
Mackerel. Lobster Sauce. Potatoes.

Two Spring Chickens Boiled. Oyster Sauce.
Lobster Patties. Sweetbreads. Ham.

Fore Quarter of Lamb. Stewed Kidneys. Curry
Rabbit. Two Ducklings.

Asparagus. New Potatoes. Peas.

Currant and Raspberry Tart. Orange Jelly.
Custards. Cabinet Pudding.

[All the Summer.]

Oyster Soup. Vermicelli Soup.

Cod's Head. Smelts. Fried Whitings.

Saddle of Mutton. Curry Oysters. Veal Olives.
Tongue. Fricassee Chickens. Lobster Salad.

Two Boiled Fowls. Oyster Sauce.

Two Wild Ducks. Two Pheasants.

Lemon Pudding. Jelly. Tart.

[All the Winter.]

Vermicelli Soup.   Ox-Tail Soup.

Turbot and Smelts.   Stewed Eels.   Soles and
Cod's Head.

Fricassee Chicken.   Oyster Patties.   Stewed
Kidneys.   Roast Sweetbreads.

Two Boiled Fowls.   Ham.   Pigeon Pie.   Saddle
of Mutton.

Three Woodcocks.   Hare.   Two Wild Ducks.
Mashed Potatoes.   Brocoli.

Apple Tart.   Orange Fritters.   Charlotte Russe.
Italian Cream.

Macaroni.   Toasted Cheese.

[All the Winter.]

Mock Turtle.   Hare Soup.   Ox-Tail Soup.

Cod's Head.   Oyster Sauce.   Smelts.   Soles.
Shrimp Sauce.   Stewed Eels.   Oyster Sauce.

Roast Turkey.   Sausages.

Brocoli.   Ham.   Sweetbreads.   Curry Lobster.
Haunch of Mutton. Brocoli. Brown Potatoes.
Pigeon Pie.   Oyster Patties.

Maintenon Cutlet.   Potatoes.   Brocoli.

Boiled Turkeys.   Oyster Sauce.

Two Woodcocks.   Hare.   Four Snipes.

Cabinet Pudding.   Apple Tart.   Charlotte Russe.
Jelly.

[All the Winter.]

BILLS OF FARE FOR FOURTEEN, EIGHTEEN, OR TWENTY PERSONS.

White Soup.   Spring Vegetable Soup.

Boiled Salmon.   Lobster Sauce.   Filletted
Lobster.   Shrimp Sauce.   Cucumbers.

Mushroom Patties.   Lobster Cutlet.   Lamb's
Cutlet, with Cucumber Sauce.   Rabbit Curry,
smothered with White Sauce.

Roast Haunch of Mutton.   Boiled Fowl and
Tongue.   Spinach.   New Potatoes.   Salad.
Duckling.   Guinea Fowl.   Asparagus.

Clear Jelly.   Italian Cream.   Marble Cream.
Strawberry Cream.

Lobster Salad.

[April to July.]

Green Pea Soup.

Broiled Salmon.   Turbot.   Lobster Sauce.
Cucumbers.

Mushroom Patties.   Lamb's Fry.   Lobster Curry.
Rissols.

Roast Saddle of Mutton.   Mayonnaise of Chicken.
Brocoli.   New Potatoes.   Roast Duck.   Peas.

Pudding.   Clear Jelly.   Italian Cream.   Macaroni.

Cheese.   Brunswick Sausage, &c.

[May to Aug.]

White Soup.   Asparagus Soup.

Boiled Salmon.   Lobster Sauce.   Cucumbers.
Filletted Soles.   Shrimp Sauce.

Mushroom Patties.   Pork Cutlets.   Oyster Curry.
Lamb's Fry.   Grenadine of Veal.

Fore-Quarter of Lamb.   Boiled Chicken and
Tongue.

New Potatoes.   Spinach.   Salad.

Larded Capon.   Roast Pigeons.   Asparagus.

Clear Jelly.   Italian Cream.   Noyau Jelly.
Macaroni.   Ice Pudding.

Brunswick Sausage, with small Salad.   Anchovies.
Cheese.

[April to July.]

Asparagus Soup.   White Soup.

Boiled Salmon.   Lobster Sauce.   Filletted Soles.
Shrimp Sauce.

Patties.   Pork Cutlets.   Lobster Ditto.
Grenadine of Veal.   Rabbit Curry.

Fore-Quarter of Lamb.   Chickens and Tongue.
Spinach.   Potatoes.   Salad.

Guinea Fowl. Pigeons. Lobster Salad. Asparagus.

Cabinet Pudding.   Punch Jelly.   Charlotte
Russe.   Clear Jelly.   Italian Cream.

[June to Sept.]

Vegetable Soup.

Turbot, with Smelts.   Shrimp Sauce.

Roast Saddle of Mutton.   Boiled Fowls.   Tongue.
Oyster Curry.   Rice.   Pork Cutlets.   Spinach.
Mashed and Brown Potatoes.   Beetroot Salad.

Cabinet Pudding.   Marmalade Tartlets.   Custards.
Macaroni.

[Nov. to March.]

APPENDIX.

———•———

MAÎTRE D'HÔTEL BUTTER.

Put a quarter of a pound of fresh butter upon a
plate, the juice of two lemons, and two large
table-spoonfuls of chopped parsley, half a tea-
spoonful of salt, and half that quantity of white
pepper ; mix all well together, and keep in a
cool place for use.

SAUCE À LA MAÎTRE D'HÔTEL.

Put eight table-spoonfuls of white sauce in a
stew-pan, with four of milk, boil it five minutes,
then stir in three ounces of maître d'hôtel butter,
stir it quickly over the fire till the butter is melted,
but do not let it boil.   This sauce should be made
at the time of serving.

POTATO BALLS.

Bake the potatoes, mash them very nicely,
make them into balls, rub them over with the

yolk of an egg, and put them into the oven or before the fire to brown. These balls may be varied by the introduction of a third portion of grated ham or tongue.

HORSE-RADISH SAUCE.

Stew an onion in a little fish-stock until it will pulp, add a tea-spoonful of grated horse-radish, and one or two spoonfuls of essence of anchovies ; beat all together over a fire ; thicken it with a little butter, and finish with a spoonful of lemon pickle or lemon juice ; vinegar may be substituted, in which case it must be mixed with the horse-radish and boiled with it, while the lemon or lemon pickle (being of a delicate flavour) should only be warmed.

ITALIAN CREAM.

Whip together for nearly an hour a quart of very thick scalded cream, a quart of raw cream, the grated rind of four lemons and the strained juice, with ten ounces of white powdered sugar, then add half-a-pint of sweet wine, and continue to whisk it until it becomes quite solid ; lay a piece of muslin in a sieve, and ladle the cream upon it with a spoon ; in twenty hours turn it carefully out, but mind it does not break ; garnish it with fruit, jelly, or with flowers.

SCOTCH BROTH.

Set on the fire four ounces of pearl barley, with three Scotch pints (or six quarts) of salt water, when it boils skim it, and add what quantity of salt beef or fresh brisket you choose, and a marrow bone or a fowl, with a couple of pounds of either lean beef or mutton, and a good quantity of leeks, cabbages or savoys, or you may use turnips, onions, and grated carrots ; keep it boiling for at least four or five hours ; but if a fowl be used, let it not be put in till just time enough to bring it to table when well done, for it must be served up separately.

MUTTON BROTH.

The best part of the mutton from which to make good broth is the chump end of the loin, but it may be made excellently from the scrag end of the neck only, which should be stewed gently for a long time (full three hours or longer, if it be large,) until it becomes tender, but not boiled to rags as it usually is ; a few grains of whole pepper, with a couple of fried onions and some turnips, should be put along with the meat an hour or two before sending up the broth, which should be strained from the vegetables, and chopped parsley and thyme be mixed in it ; the turnips should be mashed and served in a separate dish to be eaten with the mutton, with parsley-

and-butter or caper sauce. If meant for persons
in health, it ought to be strong or it will be
insipid ; the cooks usually skim it frequently, but
if given as a remedy for a severe cold, it is much
better not to remove the fat, as it is very healing
to the chest.

LEG OF MUTTON WITH OYSTERS.

Parboil some fine well-fed oysters, take off the
beards and horny parts, put to them some parsley,
minced onions, and sweet herbs boiled and chopped
fine, and the yolks of two or three hard-boiled
eggs ; mix all together, and make five or six holes in
the fleshy part of a leg of mutton, and put in the
mixture, and dress it in either of the following
ways : tie it up in a cloth and let it boil gently
two and a half or three hours according to
the size, or braise it, and serve it with a pungent
brown sauce.

TO BOIL CAULIFLOWER WITH PARMESAN.

Boil a cauliflower, drain it on a sieve, and cut
it into convenient-sized pieces, arrange these
pieces in a pudding-basin so as to make them
resemble a cauliflower on the dish, season it as
you proceed, turn it on the dish, then cover it
with a sauce made of grated parmesan cheese,

butter, and the yolks of a couple of eggs seasoned with lemon juice, pepper, salt, and nutmeg, and put parmesan grated over it ; bake for twenty minutes and brown it.

SWISS PUDDING.

In many parts of the continent, as well as throughout Switzerland, it is customary to put layers of crumbs of bread and sliced apples, with sugar between, till the dish be as full as it will hold ; let the crumbs be the uppermost layer, then pour melted butter over it, and bake.

ASPARAGUS SOUP.

Take two quarts of good beef or veal broth, put to it four onions, two or three turnips and some sweet herbs, with the white part of a hundred of young asparagus, but if old or very large at the stem half that quantity will do, and let them all simmer till sufficiently tender to be rubbed through a tammy, which is not an easy matter if they be not very young ; then strain and season it, have ready the boiled tops which have been cut from the stems, and add them to the soup ; or poach half-a-dozen eggs rather hard, have ready a hundred of asparagus heads boiled tender, boil three quarts of clear gravy soup, put into it for a

minute or two a fowl just roasted, then add a few
tarragon leaves, season with a little salt, put the
eggs and asparagus heads quite hot into the
tureen and pour the soup over them without
breaking them ; the fowl will be just as good as
before for made dishes.

SALMON CURRY.

Have two slices of salmon weighing about a
pound each, which cut into pieces of the size of
walnuts ; cut up two middling-sized onions, which
put into a stew-pan with an ounce of butter and a
clove of garlic cut in thin slices ; stir over the fire
till becoming rather yellowish, then add a tea-
spoonful of curry powder, and half that quantity of
curry paste ; mix all well together with a pint of
good broth, beat up and pass through a tammy into
a stew-pan, put in the salmon, which stew about
half-an-hour, pour off as much of the oil as possible ;
if too dry, moisten with a little more broth, mixing
it gently, and serve as usual with rice separate.
Salmon curry may also be made with the remains
left from a previous dinner, in which case reduce
the curry sauce until rather thick before putting
in the salmon, which only requires to be made hot
in it. The remains of a turbot may also be
curried in the same way, and also any kind of
fish.

PRINCE ALBERT'S PUDDING.

Put one pound of butter into a saucepan, with three quarters of a pound of loaf-sugar finely powdered, mix them well together, then add the yolks of six eggs well beaten, and as much fresh candied orange as will add colour and flavour, being first beaten to a fine paste ; line the dish with paste for turning out, and when filled with the above lay a crust over as if it were a pie, and bake it in a slow oven ; it is as good cold as hot.

CHARLOTTE RUSSE.

Line the bottom of a plain round mould with Savoy biscuits, placing them close together in a star or some device ; line the sides, placing the biscuits edgeways to make them form a compact wall, put the mould upon ice, have ready a Crême au Marasquin, adding a glass of brandy ; fill the mould as it stands on the ice, and leave it till the time of serving, when turn it over on the dish and take off the mould.

MAYONNAISE.

A cold roast fowl divided into quarters, young lettuce cut in quarters and placed on the dish with salad dressing, eggs boiled hard and cut in quarters, placed round the dish as a garnish; capers and anchovies are sometimes added.

E 2

SCOTCH MINCED COLLOP.

Take two pounds of the fillet of beef, *chopped very fine*, put it in a stew-pan, and add to it pepper and salt and a little flour, add a little good gravy, with a little ketchup and Harvey's sauce, and let it stew for twenty minutes over a slow fire ; serve up very hot, garnished with fried sippet of bread. This quantity of beef makes a good-sized dish.

COD RECHAUFFÉ.

Take any cold cod that may be left, warm up with mashed potatoes, and serve with oyster sauce poured over.

EVE'S PUDDING.

Take half-a-pound of very finely grated bread crumbs, half-a-pound of finely chopped apples, half-a-pound of currants, half-a-pound of very fine suet, six ounces of sugar, four eggs, a little nutmeg, two ounces of citron and lemon peel ; butter the mould well, and boil three hours.

HOMINY.

Boil Indian corn in milk, add sugar or salt according to taste.

KALECANNON.

Boil three or four carrots *tender,* some nice young greens, a few turnips, a few potatoes ; cut off the *outsides* of the carrots and chop them up *very fine,* also chop the greens, mash the turnips and potatoes, then place it in a melon shape to form the stripes of colours, filling up the interior of the mould with all the vegetables chopped up together with pepper and salt. Butter the mould, and boil half-an-hour.

LAMB'S HEAD AND MINCE.

Cut a lamb's head in half, boil and then brown in a Dutch oven or with a salamander ; mince liver and dish up together.

RICE BLANCMANGE.

Boil rice in milk, put into a mould, and let stand until cold.

SCOTCH MUTTON BROTH.

Make a good brown stock of a small shin of beef, with vegetables, carrots, turnips, onions and celery ; when sufficiently boiled the vegetables must be taken out *whole,* and the soup seasoned with pepper and salt and a little cayenne to taste ;

also a little Harvey's sauce and ketchup ; then fry
some mutton cutlets, the quantity required for the
number, a pale brown, add them to the soup with
the vegetables cut up small.

SWISS PUDDING.

Butter your dish, lay in it a layer of bread
crumbs grated very fine, then boil four or five
apples very tender, add a little butter, nutmeg,
and fine sifted sugar, mix all up together and lay
on the bread crumbs, then another layer of the
crumbs, then add pieces of fresh butter on the
top, and bake in a slow oven for a quarter of
an hour, until it become a delicate brown ; it may
be eaten hot or cold.

SPANISH PUDDING.

One pound of flour, and one table-spoonful of
good yeast to be put in a basin, melt half-a-pound
of butter in a little milk, add it to the flour and
yeast, and mix them together ; then take three
eggs—yolks and whites—with a *little salt*, and
well beat them ; when well beaten frisk them into
the butter, mix the dough well up till it will leave
the basin and spoon quite clear, let it stand to rise
for an hour, then roll it up with six ounces of
powdered sugar, and a tea-spoonful of powdered

cinnamon, and half-an-ounce of candied orange-
peel, and half-an-ounce of citron cut very fine, to
be served with sauce of clarified sugar, with orange-
flower water poured over it about half-an-hour
before sent to table.

STEAK À LA SOYER.

The rump-steak to be broiled and to be dressed
with pepper, salt, cayenne and flour, all in a dredge-
box together ; keep constantly turning the steak
and dredging it ; chop up one small shalot, put
it in a stew-pan with a little ketchup, when the
steak is sufficiently done add a little butter to it,
strain the sauce through a small sieve, and serve
up very hot.

SPANISH SALAD DRESSING.

One tea-spoonful of water, half a tea-spoonful
of pepper, ditto of salt, two wine-glasses of oil,
about a dessert-spoonful of very strong vinegar,
all well mixed together. To make this salad
thoroughly good, some sweet herbs should be
added, but chopped very fine.

Bradbury & Evans, Printers, Whitefriars.